PLANES

I love the look of planes and the idea of how a plane flies. The more I learn about it the better I feel; while I still may not like it, I have a sense of what is really happening.

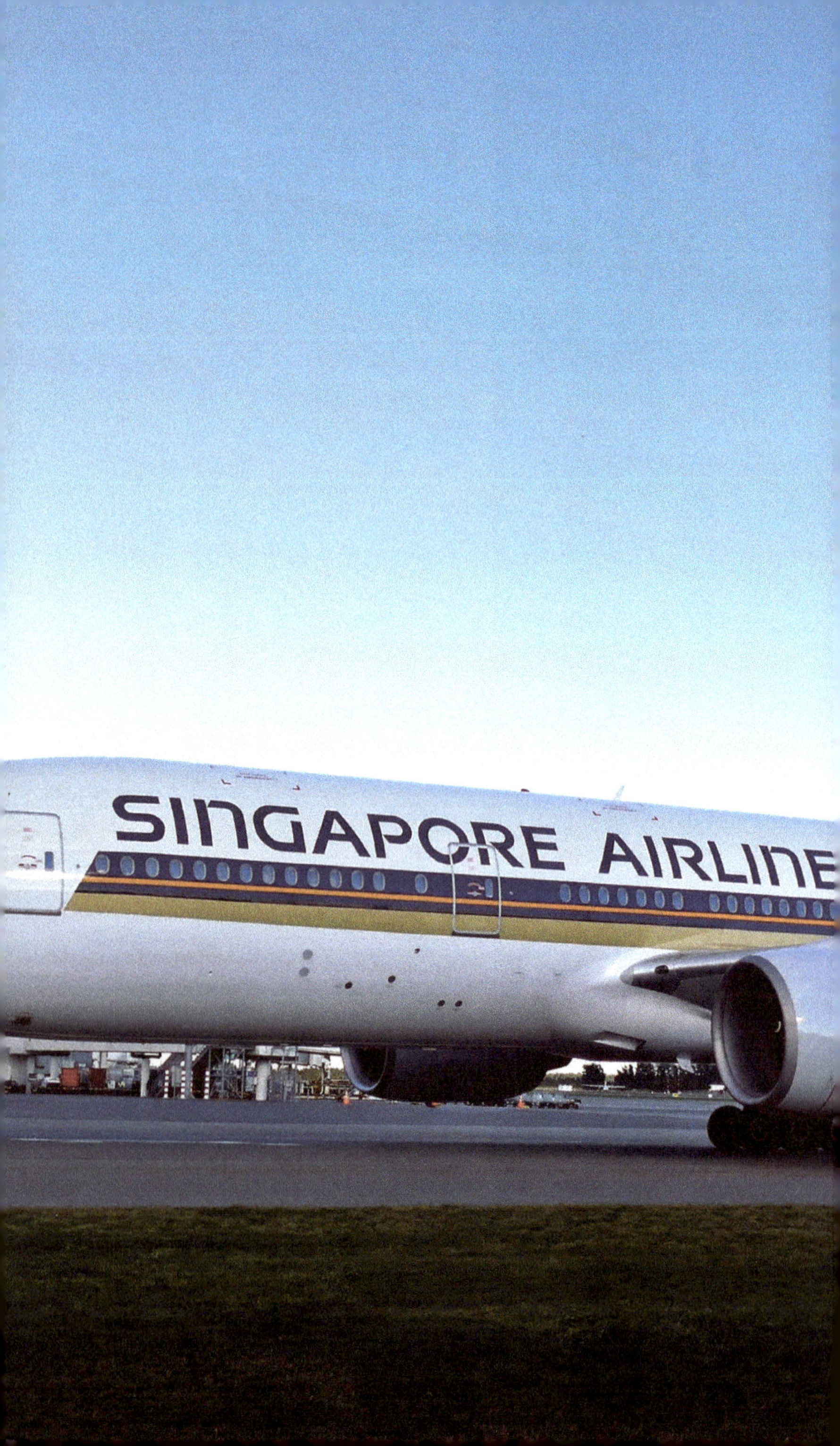
SINGAPORE AIRLINE

CPSIA information can be obtained
at www.ICGtesting.com
Printed in the USA
BVHW021534060819
555210BV00020B/321/P